ISBN: 978-1-952055-51-5

Library of Congress Control Number: 2023934642

Sometimes I am a Destroying Angel ©2023 by **Lindsey Frances Pellino**. Published in the United States by V.A. Press. Not one part of this work may be reproduced without expressed written consent from the author. For more information, please write V.A. Press, 643 South 2nd Street, Milwaukee, WI 53204 U.S.A.

Dedicated to Saint – a true angel

"O TO BE CAST FROM THE GARDEN AGAIN AND FOREVER"

John Balaban, from "Atomic Ghost"

TABLE OF CONTENTS

sometimes i am an angel	1
saturn return	2
god's own glow	3
glacier	5
pathetic	6
the menu	7
inaugural	8
new year's eve	9
2030	10
beach revelation	11
lightning	12
genius	13
six of swords	14
one small beast	16
suicide is my child	17
o death	18
order of the solar temple	20
paleolithica	21
self, a narrative	22
on the flock of headless lambs in the cemetery	24
heaven is a siren	26
zeno's bow	27
ozymandias	28
kangaroo	29
to the bottom of things	30
pikadon	31
brundlefly	33
hologram sacrifice	34
do not be afraid	36
at god's funeral	37
hibakusha	38
whiplash	39
the life and death of matter	40
holocene halcyon days	42
fire and water	43
pangea elegy	44
pangea paean	45
griefblood oracle	46
ornithomancy	48
approaching him	49

cemetery walk	50
mourning star	51
the bunker	52
protection	54
traffic on everest	56
wrath	57
burial burial	58
saint judas	59
i'm so glad i came but i can't wait to leave	61
otzi	63
the incredible shrinking god	64
east	65
if loving the bomb is right, then we have to want to be wrong	67
human nature triptych	69
adam / / / atom	71
1997	72
madonna lactans	74
katabasis	76
what we talk about when we talk about garbage	77
as above, so below	79
two and a half minutes	80
the broadcast	81
dove and olive	82
the body parts	83
theft of fire	85
ashes	86
possum skull ode	88
the tower	89
the star	90
the rock under isaac	91
pax atomica	93
angelus novus	96
sméagol's elegy	97
the last oasis	98
mary at nagasaki	99
SISENEG	101

sometimes i am an angel

sometimes i am an angel.
sometimes i read poetry
to the dying woman in
her parents' farmhouse.

the eyes, the window,
the soul. all shut up
inside me. a ball
of snakes in a
gordian knot.

death, i hope you are the knife.
i hope you are the angel i am,
sometimes. her daughter
is looking me in the eye,
like she can see a wing.

i skip words like *dead*
and *dying*, when reading
her the poems. but i say
words like *winter, ocean*.

stuffed in bottles, corked,
sealed. the angel moves
the hands to turn the page.

saturn return

the black bear racing to the lakeside
to douse her cubs in muddy water.
i wonder if there is enough dread
in her heart to hope they drown.

the fires and their smokes smooth the trees —
pinecones bursting like gunshots, like bombs.

she can feel it in her heart, the vermin
once cloistered in shelters of dirt,
as the sun vanished into dust and sulfur.
lizards gave birth, ate their own eggs,
then starved.

i have no children to eat.

this is where all roads end:
a bony cub, splashing,
while a dormant creature
waits for its turn.

god's own glow

everything is a vibration,
some more violent than others.

god smiles & it's a radiant smile
the waves beam its hot hot heat
onto the bodies of thousands of babies
until they curdle into shadow.

he smiles & my popcorn pops
& he smiles & the universe shivers
its mirage of static & he smiles
contact lights, big bang
was just a smile.

all the tight buds of atoms collapse
like a pearl onion under thumb
just a press with force & it collapses.

i'm getting darker by the sunlight
baking my skin & my retinas
are scoured by god's smiling
big white teeth - he must eat only bleach!

my head is buzzing like an ever-ringing doorbell
hooked up to a frying mouse by some frayed wires &
i could go for some electroshock therapy right now &
get smiled on by a big bright god & his big white teeth right now

or i could swallow some uranium pills
& everyone will say i have an inner glow
as my skin sloughs off in droves
& my pelvis will bottom out
& my jaw will fall off
because god has favored on me,
and they all ask me if he has hidden
things in the world for us to find,

or if he's hidden them so we never can?
but i just smile &
smile

glacier

the ice retreats its pleats
up the skin of the mountain:
the pile of italian corpses in the alps,
a nest of antlers, swollen with ticks of anthrax
sporing out their daggers.

this is the world, ending,
for me. i am breathing the pollen of the dead.
i am infected with the tomb,
melting, rivulets and streams of iron water
rushing past.

an apocalypse is an opened eye,
a path of sight, a revelation.
whip the clouds out of the sky
to reveal a sun. and in the sun
contains the core of its devotion
towards its demise. it is born
to burst. the glacier is born
to melt.

up drags the spent fuel rods,
clogged with bentonite,
next comes the army bases,
then the fishing wire, then the cave paintings,
then more copses of neanderthal campsites,
bones scattered by the retreat,
the ice performs its osteomancy
at an invisible pace.

and our legacy, simply
a thin sheen of microplastics,
strontium. one razored slice
in the strata, followed by
rock, and by rock, and by rock.

pathetic

my heart's limp beat
like a dead fish, downstream,
from all the blood in the streets.

what i feel is hunger for comfort.
when i blink, my eyes are dry.

it's so easy to slip into stillness
with the mask of enlightenment.

apathy pools into detachment
a dog circling its bed in the grass.
stir the yin and the yang into
grey slush. call it a day.
take my melatonin,
fall asleep in the pool.

i'm not afraid of the bombs
falling, i'm afraid that when
they fall,
i will yawn.

atrophied from the electric current of terror,
atrophied from the electric current of splendor,
i float through the fog.

i close my eyes.
they do not open.
they do not need to.

the menu

our charred weather —
a holocaust of atmospheres.
sand + carrion air
licks dust bowls clean of each grub & gleaming morsel:

salmon braised in boot black,
charcuterie board of foreskins, fish scales,
snakeskin sausage casing,
stuffed w/ cicada wings,
apple seeds, benedictine,
shale oil cocktail w/ phosphorus rim,
the cake that marie let them eat,
eucharist s'more, poached tumor,
pickled cornea of god's third eye,
the glistening carcass of the moon,
vinegar egg buried under soil for 100 years
yet still
still
it hatches, is hatching.

what beast awakens, slouches his elbows on the table,
toward the feast?
                             our starving hearts, their
thick purple pumps - salivate // blood.
salvation // savages holy water.

radium girls lick their paintbrush tips,
their tongues of glowing blades
carve us a slice.

inaugural

XI.VIII.MMXVI

the blood in our hearts is a rubicon torrent.
julius stands at the bank.
the horses will not pass, they hesitate,
knowing they cannot step into this river again.

in the sky, thunder quakes
birds in their flocks,
spanning heavens with their wings,
thrown up into the æther like dice.

they rain to the ground,
julius picks one up.
what can this pattern mean,
he ponders, as beast by beast they fall.

the horses will not eat,
they run from the water.
they lay on the ground as if waiting
for a symphony fire
to swallow them.

now is long past the point of divining the skies,
says julius, bird in his fist like a scepter.

he guts the thing, spills innards on the road,
and waits for a map to arise
in this utterly rudderless world.

new year's eve

for once i'd like the end of the year not to feel like
a funeral for the whole world, even if all we're doing
is spinning, dragging ourselves against the emptiness
in circles around a star, so what's the point of
the arbitrary death, then sudden rebirth?
midnight pops like a beer can tab
but out pours the flat, and the fizzles,
all across the already stained carpet.

we enter sparse winter, touch snow-soaked grave dirt
with our bare feet, pass around memories of embers,
wait for the green to explode and make us feel young
and fresh and immortal again, that first rainbow bud
punching death in the face. part of me is still stuck
kissing the mirror just to feel less lonely, six years ago,
toasting a barren glass to the air. if this eve is
a funeral, then every day is a ceremony, a grieving,
even the spring,
and yet—

2030

my lungs are bell tongues,
clanging alarm - the in breath out breath -
sharp as shards. this horizon's lips
snarl over the edge.

the shrill frill of a spider lily
in its white web of fronds -
i see them atomize
in the sunlight.

i see them drown,
as a hot fish carcass
confettis itself,
sinks its fine bone anchor.

a carrion of islands. a siren.
is it any use to collect them
at the perfumery?

when they vulture our shipwreck
and uncork the centuries old bottle of now,

out will curdle
the ringing stench
of a world gone dewy -
humid as a tyrannosaurus maw,
cracking open &
spilling its swamp.

beach revelation

oxygen poison planetesimal   the stygian night for multitude millenia
over which no fowl nor beast nor creature roamed nor roiled
the deep blue birth that swirled in silent dust around
a just-born sun   spewing helical party streamers

the iron core flow   cataclysm spins   the mountains
pulverized to granules   sand does not rejoice
upon compression into a stained glass window.

the oceans and their rumblings   blue whales   pink jellies
sea stars   manatee   krill   kelp   barracuda   coral
over which the gulls sharply shriek   their tinny aubade
of untallied mornings before featherless bipeds
ate special k breakfast cereal at a particle board table.

i do not mourn for these epochs   seamless shift
smooth and steady molasses universe dripping its black eye
throughout   gets cold and cold and i do not cry   the sea
its glass face ripples in a peerless form each moment
i do not mourn its shimmering face   a blink   and i think
to myself   not to dwell on the stagnant, their illusions
of plastic potted houseplants to trick the brain into living forever
in a supermarket aisle with a fat baby in the front compartment

but instead drift   to the ceaseless   the wave and the ocean
all crest all trough   the mountain dispersed and shared
the death blanket night sky   tucks it all in

lightning

who's isaac more afraid of:
the father, or the stone?

i can admit to the mist
of paleolithic, that the thunder's

lowing breath reignites
my fallowed ganglia.

the fractal shattering,
white clamoring, bright

in its raw hot slash. fear
is a burning of nerves

and isaac's afraid
of the heat.

genius

a genius releases a devil from a bottle
and it's the mother's fault, for she
was the chicken, the egg.

i say, mother. but i mean,
earth's fruits are a delight, and a curse,
this whole planet's a big frothing brothel.
i say, fruits. i mean, men.

man is a thing, woman is a force,
my god my god, my kingdom for a horse.

i say genius, i mean, the boundary of hell,
mined for some fresh gem, as they wipe
their brow of soot, to present their findings
to all of humanity.

man is the fire, woman is the air,
look upon my works,
ye mighty, and despair.

but the children -
none know what they say, nor do.
someone, forgive them,
for their knowledge beyond sense
and ignorance beyond mercy.

meanwhile, in the pool of void,
sits the headstones worn blank
by wind and fallen pines.

six of swords

when the body dies of thirst,
the tongue cracks its thunder

the face canyons its cheeks
the hollow haunches

evaporates, accumulates
beds of dust. the oxygen

grows heavy in the stream,
the burden too great to migrate.

a desert of convulsions
shrinks us to our pits,

dessicated marrow
to ash and to ash.

an intersection of veins
clogged at the crossing,
the blood cooling down.

dead before she realizes
she's turned to stone.

concentrate the soul to a morsel,
undistinguished from the fields of sand
rippling their false flag oases
in dry, stale air.

o our consecrated skeletons
ye bleached bones
found by the workers
in their hasty graves.

when the body dies of thirst,

it is never an accident.

thugs kick jugs,
gut waters out
in an arc of eden.

slithers back into the ground
to coax itself to vapor
in the glare of our incurious sun.

what is the divine purpose
of a girl dying in the night,
organs failing and fleeing?

what is the equation
if the generated output
is the corpse of a child,
laying on the cement floor,
bound in aluminum?

when the body dies of thirst,
it does not die of thirst.

it dies of agony.
it dies of canonization.
it dies of transubstantiation,
transmuted, mote by mote,
to a divine plane as useless
as an emptied cup.

one small beast

[*distant atavistic groan*]

the strumming of crickets and heat

i sit

on the gravel pile

in the cage.

the moon is the fat white belly of a frog laid back in the swamp mud.

when the air is this thick,
a baby cries and a bird cries
urgent and terrified
up to the stars.

pure data - need -
and the unmet quiet
of a growing dark.

suicide is my child

on the playground, we couldn't go to the ER
when she sliced her fingers off on a razor blade
that some asshole glued to the monkey bars

because then they'd see her, the way
she was being raised, on iced oat milk vanilla lattes
and the empty toner dust from all the cartridges
i stacked on my desk that i kept meaning
to bring to staples to recycle but nothing matters.

so i just kissed the raw knuckles as her eyes streamed
their river tears into her powder blue gingham romper.
she tells me not to bother and goes to sleep on the couch.

does she know i love her?

the moment of her conception,
the apple tree heaved its tired, tired blossoms
to the soil. the arms of a thousand toilers
collapsed the mountains to mud.

another great thing about her is that she never gets sad
about the bins upon bins of discarded memorabilia
at the goodwill store, including the custom hummingbird
cross-stitch embroidered to someone named jacqueline.

Suicide grows up to be the mouth-inflated
pale pink balloon taped to the senior center
welcome sign with a bandaid. i am proud of her
as she flutters so weakly in the breeze, the wind
echoing up the coast from a leftover hurricane.

i hope she waits for me in heaven.
i took so long to meet her maker.

o death

o motley technicolor dreamboat
o body bags, o bog bodies, o ossuaries, o pyramids
your great black wings cast shadows over ruins.
i want to feel you slip silver coins over my eyes.
i want to float down the river styx like a stillborn baby moses.

o death, you scare me.
please do not tell me there is an afterlife or
i will just kill myself right now.

with your fungus bouquet + carmine rivulets,
i can sense you,
not hiding, not waiting, but shouting *ta-dah*
every time my eyes close.

my eyes will close a final time,
or will i die with them open,
until they put barbed wire contact lenses
on my corneas so they don't spring open,
for the domain of surprise is yours alone?

you blue careful thing, you make everything still,
the universe bereft of shimmering wavelengths + hula hooping strings.
you make it so placid and flat and then just exist forever by yourself.
maybe you are a buddha enlightened and knowing we are all the same
and you are just the mechanism that makes it happen.

o death, you god of entropy, i've been working so hard to stay the same but that's part of the problem. i've been working so hard to find someone that makes me crazy, makes me literally crazy, makes me froth at the mouth and all that heat, all that heat taken from the sun is just killing me faster, killing the universe faster.

the smallest of spaces obsidian thin between my inhales and exhales
i feel you rising to the surface, hovering the buzzard wings, maw agape,
abyssopelagic stretching your jaw across my whole soul.

will you spit, or will you swallow?

o death, do you love me
when i pull petals off flowers?
mindlessly tear grass from sod as if to tempt you,
to show you all the little things i can do to please you?

what will it take for you to drop your cloak,
reveal your miraculous backside, and
leave me blinded by the bomb of your dark?

order of the solar temple

climbing through the equinox
the bodies lay down, in a rose of mirrors.
the petals - portals - bloom an arthritic furl.
        He forgives me, He forgives me not.
        He forgives me, He forgives me not.
pluck body by body until wrenched, whole-less.

mechanisms for miracles
paraded before their eyes
like shadows, they dart past
the whispering cave mouth
[who lashes its burning tongue
at the wicked passerby]

cursed corneas,
their earthly gauze
filters away the hiding
        god god god
emmanuel! a fire of stars!
the eye is merely a blister
ripened by His brightness.

the antichrist, full of splinters,
blazes in a plume of smoke
at the glance of His solar glare.

sing to us, psychopomp of fire,
to a mirrored room.
the brightness of a rose
curdles sin into oblivion.
furnace, cradle our headstones
on Your blazing knees.

little bodies -
let the Dog Star shroud you
in its lullaby of flame.

paleolithica

tectonic plates unfurl deep shadows,
casting whirls of stone onto mountains.
mountains then slowly climb and drift;
each rift cuts coasts in two, in four, more
pour out, like slivers from the blow.
panthalassa flowing, molten iron,
unity undone. those coastline seams
seem to be on purpose: god loves puzzles,
but he loves to smash too and undo us:
tongues of babel, towers of gomorrah,
peeking under pandora's dress to see
what monsters come lurching out beneath her.

when we birthed ourselves from dirt,
did we shed our genome on command?
                no.
we, people from rust, planet of specks,
oxidize our lungs on accident. breath
is an afterthought, is a beforethought.
no ancestry on shore waving hands
at their progeny as pangea fled.

we so crave
to trace the shadows of our skin on the earth.
but history shuffles the ages
like a deck of cards,
like a house of cards,
fragile in the wind.

self, a narrative

my malady is a rotted cornucopia on the curio cabinet.

but what's the ending?
turn the page
blank
blank
blank
like the sky of an apocalypse
yanks the tablecloth away,
scrapes heaven raw

but what's the ending?
underneath my skull
is a brain
and in the brain
must be another
a matryoshka, et cetera

but what's the ending?
the meaning —
scraped from the bottom
of the crumb collector:
the constant taunting threnody,
shrieking since birth.
this parcel of cortices
devoted to her altar
that she carved herself
out of the cave of my skull.

in the end, my malady cannot be burned,
extracted, exhumed, devoured.
she is immune to each curse and hex i cast,
i have tried to concuss until she cracked
in two, or even chipped, reduced,
just one mote of ash.

but she just rocks and laughs,
rocks and laughs, her lure
still undissected,
in the nest of my throat.

on the flock of headless lambs in the cemetery

acid rain, kiss my brows.
mother, mother nature,
absolve me into particulates.
my moss crumb brain;
sweet pudding the lichen sips.

the mountain shares itself to the world
until it is sand.

heaven is a flock of smooth doves,
carving out tunnels in the nimbus clouds,
worms in the loam.

heaven is a herd of headless lambs,
silent, yearning for shepherd,
as chrysanthemums turn their red faces
toward the blazing sun.
budded on earth, bloomed in heaven
gone but not
    [   ]

caregivers with their sheers,
sisyphus as psychopomp.
the tree butchered to the stump,
rings bare, ready for the weathering of
the slowest storm imaginable
whose thunderhead sits
on the throne of the horizon
year after year
inching toward the shore.

how our diamonds will melt
the babies in their cocoons,
stagnant. years are a guillotine.

a moldering apple at the root

spews its nitrogen,
dreams of being the tree it feeds.
and in the separate afterlife for lamb heads,
all resting on golden platters,
death ties the off-white plastic lobster bib around her neck.

god is ravenous for more angels. death lifts the cloche.
the tender cheek, turned and turned again, to soften.
a menu of obituaries. under mourning veils —

the salt, tears, spit coalesce into grief.
the weeping veal swallowed the only way they can be:
whole.

heaven is a siren

when i die i'm gonna dream forever.

i thrash my birdsong
against the cobalt sky.

the glass windowpane i fly into
is just a mirror, as all things are.

a constant vision of a perfect world
waves from that mirror

in the funhouse. i turn,
watching its image dart to smoke.

zeno's bow

i awake tomorrow at fifty years
unalive, like stone or water,
the same-ish, just becoming smaller
parts of the self/ish. time as humidity
ceaseless fervor, blood sponge of tongue
clogged and begs, pants, the mare in heat—
me. i awake another tomorrow
in the funeral, that organ haunted word,
orchard of darkened faces, deliberately
turning from the sun, like terrible flowers.
it is time to love winter.

ozymandias

for terri ardor

i've pictured the empty auditorium from ten story buildings,
bottles of pills, even firearms, the oven gas.
my last words carved into ice, safe from melting,
since there are no more troys left to burn.
still, there is no one clapping.
you know what they say:
everyone's a critic.

but i've had the road to damascus moment, with my helium mask bolted on.
it's the only effective pain free way, i've heard it said, i've heard it screamed
by sirens of anxiety. the world is ending in fire and ice, with bangs and whimpers,
so what is the difference between melting glaciers, freezing lava?
that's the set up. and the punchline is as follows:
my feet fossilize as i crawl and lurch toward a white bursting star,
to someplace cool and damp, the wall of a cave.
i drag my kneecaps into glass.

but it's too late. this desert is a field of poppies stuck in a root of lightning.
i'm winding down in the debris. pulse of heat. flesh fused to the tanks of atmosphere.
deep breaths inevitable.
my third eye vomits on the rocks. this isn't funny anymore. but lot's wife is laughing
in the corner, and she says, *this is the only real way to live forever.*
and she's right, i think, as the wall of fire stretches the horizon away.

kangaroo

a nerve of soft pink pearl,
translucent, pulsing,
shucks off the mother,

slimes across her gut.
one harsh reach,
a desert of flesh.

barely a breath
to expand fish-fine lungs,
though it lunges
on instinct grip,
mucus glob, a blood-slip,
alive, toward milk.

the world dances, is a dance,
unknowingly knowing the knowledge
of wound regenesis, of heart arithmetic,
of the winding down,
but does *it* know?
as it crawls, where is the terror
of false step, plummet to earth?
is there space in the clockwork
for spark?

but look, my hands begin to wither
of their own accord,
no electron out of place,
in their deep dark orchestra.
the nerves point their compass
and i follow, hypnotized,
thinking & knowing
without reason.

to the bottom of things

underneath the road is the dirt
underneath the house is the grass

underneath the thin skin
marbled in jaundice and velvet
spits a man

underneath his blanket is a jar of limbs
anywhere he knelt,
under it an altar.

the woman in the wheelchair with the wild hair holds a baby doll
both knowing and not that it is a decoy.

underneath the x-ray fog is a sharp diamond
underneath that diamond is a scared girl

underneath the girl is the dirt
underneath the dirt is a family of roots
tapping at a door

the door will open and reveal the road
and when that day comes

i will be underneath a bruised blue sky
flush with black, mottled plum,
fire bursts of stars and pinnacles.

i will be underneath a thousand pulsating worms,
worms that know that all boundaries are illusions,
and one worm is a thousand is a million.

underneath those worms is the house under the grass
at the end of the road. and the door behind me
will close as gently as an eye.

pikadon

skyscrapers bow to the dirt, steel girdles snapped by this
runaway child i have left to feral scissor chase the earth
with her wild fingers and branches

the ant and its curlicue antenna traverses static landscape
soldier of fortune   dirt widow   witnessed the birth
of the sun an inch from its hill

and the child eyes my breasts   my milk   clean and eden flow
then my heels   the tide has latched to my ankles
with teeth foam and gnashed until my stumps have struck me

daphne deep into the fulgurite   my child scrapes up my side
to reach the fountain   it was once a part of
when past the cervix it lurked in my waters   and the shimmering ants

their glittering pincers   careening   in and out
to take what amino and enzyme they need in this world
i cradle the flash   my mother arms   my withered stumps

snow ash so dainty and sirius white   the radium ants collect it too
for their colonies and they take pride in their huts and coliseums
their cathedrals their colossus their behemoth and one day

i know when we crash down into our ooze they will evolve
and become the gods of the planet and they will feel within
their bellies the stirring of an imp

screaming to be born   they will build it with green bones
calcified in the hadean fields   swathes of elegant algae
a-bloom with the neptunian winds ever howling   roaring the breath of god

my child tugs at the rags of my skirt
her cute eyes   steel brimstone hair flame halo
milk teeth coated in fantastic dust
she whispers deep   in my ovaries   commands another sister to hatch

slide down the winding fallopian faustian pathways
squarely plop on the beach and to once again splatter the shadows
of a billion puny creatures on to the cement
in a black flash of void.

brundlefly

the male anglerfish bites the female on the back.
she wears him like a wart.
he dries up, puckers to scab,
his shrunken testicles,
withered, dangle on her face.
she grows alone, as one.

this is what i've been told
to be love:
an amalgamation. a latching,
vice suck till it's a swollen tick,
it's two people both spitting in a vase
swilling it around
taking a swig.

if geena davis got in that transporter with jeff goldblum
that'd be true love.
one fused graft, wet scoured clay,
slapped together and kilned,
throbbing up spittle from a tongue-clogged mouth,
always kissing.

hologram sacrifice

i burnt a sims family today as an offering to god.
each patch of fire was identical —
smokeless, they compressed into ash piles,
then instantaneously converted into urns.

yet it wasn't close enough
to the bloody things required
to make god favor on you.

i cut off prosthetic limbs,
butchered roadkill,
kicked dead guys in the crotch,
built a robot that projects
lifelike images of lambs
being put feet first
into meat grinders.

but god still says:
not good enough.

no approximations,
no facsimiles,
no tofu throat slit,
no bullshit.

he wants me upended on that spike,
splinters in my liver,
eyes clouded over and ovaries burst at the seams.

he wants me to prove something
about the weakness of the flesh

by saying it doesn't matter
if all my teeth explode, if my skin boils up,
or if i'm decapitated for my misdeeds.

it doesn't matter if this tsunami
pins me to the ocean floor,
because the bacteria-sized part of me,
the part that's bioluminescent, ethereal,
wearing a silver and blue wizard hat,
is the *real* me.

not the pink slobbering worm-laced brain
that uses electrical grunts
to swing my arms and stomp my feet.

that's all gonna be taken away someday
and god really loves it
when you do it yourself.

do not be afraid

do not be afraid...said the angel to the human...cowered under his school desk...as he shits his pants...a quintilian fractal rotating eyes...*shriek, ye eye wheel, shriek!*....an iris on every atom...shoot their irradiated beams...explode the doves...in fits of white ash...fear not the reign of heaven...rain of heaven...burst...and shimmer....stratosphere of diamond dust...repulse us...alien air...unbreathable...our poisoned lungs and skeletons...blinded...we don't look away...can't...even when god just wants...to show us...his backside...we tear our hair...moses...how did you do it...did you squint...wear sunglasses...by the pool...would heaven be terrifying...boiling...a sun of infinite pleasure...fusion...more painful than fission...will rebrth...hurt more than...birth?

at god's funeral

i'm going to be sitting in the back pew,
making a scene during the eulogy.
they turn around to tut at me,
as i shriek, obscenely, like a car crash.

god looks so serene in the coffin
with a big stupid cloud face
that isn't human or planet.

a lump of matter and spirit.
people are weeping
but they can't say
in a better place.

he's nowhere anymore
like all those kids he trapped in wells
until their bodies seeped their bile.
he's a botched tracheotomy
a raccoon in the bike lane
brain matter splattered.
dumb and numb
slung into a box.

maybe they can believe
that this is orchestrated
by an intelligent entity, benevolently,
and tremble before him.
as if he made us any other way,
our subatomic filaments quiver
their ringing bells, every nanosecond
the constant tremble, all the way down.

but look, there's god,
being lowered into sod
leaving a hole in the wake
for any old thing to fill.

hibakusha

o ever the phoenix that rises, sung of ash, the swathes of flame,
reaches through newly anointed and dazzling—

there are the ones who are stuck
after death, before genesis,
in the hybrid plane
of ever renewing scars, bent claws,
fingers reverting to fish.

o the sunburns, o the animated carcass,
weep their glowing tears. no men to absorb them, as wives.
if you take them on, they will turn you out.

your heart roasts, everything falls in clumps and shucks
the quivering oyster flesh: pink, then red, then black.

their babies stiffened with healing, over-skinned,
womb knitting an armor, as if to say *please do not harm this baby,
it is so weak, and the winds are so bright.*

o charnel womb, o hephastian tomb,
in which we pack our bricks of dead fruit:
the furnace few, who gather in church basements,
mummify in balaclavas, wear sunglasses by the light of new moons,
who've been disrobed by the holy spirit,
whose translucent skeletons echo,
whose tangled limbs fold to swollen lotuses,
who fall prey to flies and gnats,
who heard the clarions whine and the sirens of heaven shrill and spill their fire,
who stood like salt pillars at the pandemonium gates,
who condemn st michael's flaming sword and he who cast the first stone —

they, the heralds of dawn:
the only ones with the birthright
to raise the sun.

whiplash

she brakes into telephone pole,
foot down with the weight
of a severed elevator crate.
the rims clamp slammed
down the gallows of her calf.

glowstick of neck, overzealously cracked,
the bright waters of flame and
streetlamp pool at the collarbones
for the camera to lap at.

bundled spine as a tether between here

and not here.

what she wanted was to stop —
slowly, with overflowing time.
though the body does its destiny,
launches rockethearted,
trajectory vow, domino body,
following orders all the way down
to neon red asphalt.
        [the videotapes you were warned about,
        footage enough to make you stand still
        for the rest of your life.]

she was the only one,
wrenched, angel of reversals,
who saw the past,
over her shoulders,
rushing up to claim her.

the life and death of matter

"I'm just a womb, standing in front of a fascist, asking for the same rights as a corpse"
-Marcia Belsky

death is a dry labor. we know this.
desert doulas with their speculums of ice

to melt the passageways'
slippery wet slits.

my body es su casa,
when we die it all falls down.

the afterlife becomes
no where else to go.

her latex gloves at the crown,
wider & wider & wider.

life, its wet labor, its
swamp fog, tidal pool,

getting siphoned
by a big fat straw

like a mosquito proboscis
in the medulla oblongata

into the various flasks
you don't need anymore.

the blood from my brain
is just the grand canyon in reverse.

what i mean is,
eve is still pushing

and there is no third option.
there is no other bear trap.

no other stomach to cut open
again & again & again.

my corrosive movements,
though slow, will collect,

will one day be enough
to gouge your heart out.

will one day be enough
to free my body from this

endless back and forth
between rock & hard place

and i can just sit, floating,
lotus position, in a stasis.

the cradle - its lightning cracks -
above the darkness.

would someone just give
that whole thing a shove

and let the abundance, abyss?
can one day my stillness

be more than alternate reality,
drawn on paper, admired in secret,

folding the sheet right before
you open the door?

holocene halcyon days

every year we pass
the birthday of the last
living dinosaur. so i peel apart
the shale to hunt for
fossilized birthday hat,
party horn.

the arbitrarily lit candles
before the wishless raptor skull.
with his skinless smile,
the kinless ultimate,
their flames fueled by
his family's liquified remains,
who left him behind
to the solitude of personhood.

when we watch the last tiger
mortify, order baked ziti catering trays
(serves 15-20)
for the funeral reception,
i place my mourning in the dirt.

the last human on earth
throws a birthday party,
knowing adam's loneliness.
the grass on the last remaining bridge
grows thirty feet tall. her fingers
pinch the flames. she sings a birthday dirge.
she wishes for the earth to sing back.
instead, it laughs.

fire and water

a clear bolt from pendulous skies
shoots into dry brush

or

a deliberate snap of prometheus's fingers,
divine secret carved from the sun?

us so unwieldy,
we blister ourselves to plasma,
we scald, we eat species to their bone char.

on mars, at the same time we discovered fire,
there stirred salted waters.

enough to flood the sparking
enough to calm
the oncoming eureka.

pangaea elegy

she wanted to go somewhere exotic.

thick with swamps and seaweed, where we could watch aurora from the tip of a tidal wave, surrounded by ocean mist and a seizure of flora.

we live on a desert, a scorched farmhouse on the edge of an edge of an edge. the only oasis is an orbiting dive bar called Watering Hole. i think that's a dumb name.

i told her of the perfect place, one cerulean gulp, floods abundant, centralized jungles, not very popular.

she remembered reading back in school that their moon was a gleaming, silver, swollen coin. *what a view they must have had*, she said, *i want to see.*

we went diving, swam through cathedrals, giant clocks, castles, old parks, monuments. there weren't a lot of fish. when we ate dinner at a restaurant called Humid, i told her i felt bad for the people.

we were floating in their catacombs, marveling at their dereliction.

she scoffed. *what do you expect? they couldn't live forever. by the time they came around, 99% of the species that ever lived were already extinct.* true, i said, but think of how much work they put into their cities, into their world.

she rolled her eyes, *this place started out as one big ocean, what's the big deal if it ends up that way? besides, their star is going to implode and boil the whole lot up in a couple more million years and it will be just as dry as home. come on, let's go to the museum before it closes.*

we left and walked through a dinky tourist trap, about daily home life of the local populations, mating habits, entertainment, etc. it killed enough time before nightfall. we rented a boat and went out to sea. magnetic sunlight whipped in colored ribbons, reflecting its wild dance on the water.

above was home, somewhere unseeable and tiny. and glowing brightly, half the moon. i thought she'd be annoyed that it wasn't full, but she turned to me and said *isn't it beautiful?*

pangaea paean

i wanted to go somewhere exotic.

nowhere dry and desiccated like home, just a molted skin left to bake in the hot white sun. i've only been to a swimming pool once in my life. it was a thin puddle of scum, but splashing in it felt like velvet. i dreamt in liquid, envied fish.

most people aren't like me. they like the arid landscape, pillars of sand and all that. but that planet's a bruise, i said, a burly distended wound. and she asked *are you romanticizing the end of their world?*

i'd rather love something than be afraid of it. and besides, it's not theirs. the universe sang its song in the shape of a blue marble and the critters worked on it, and all the ice melted into turbulent currents, and the hurricanes swirled their goliath whirls, while the people were swept away by rainfall as auspicious prisms haloed overhead. they got to feed the fish and maybe compose a coral reef.

she toyed with her food, took entropy personally. *i'd rather live on our wasteland forever as a carcass in salt. i don't want to change.* do not be afraid, i told her, it's what we were born to do.

griefblood oracle

every day, a new grief.
the cyclical dawn yawns me.
again? i ask the rising sun.
again, says the sun,
not knowing its inevitable nova.

i put the explosions on the top-most shelf,
let it pool the dust + skin particulates
from the stale air.

but now with these bulls
creutzfeld-jacking off all over the place,
their reckless horns a-smash
in our china shop planet,
up on high, the damoclean glow
sits its snowflake on our
rapidly thawing tongues.

and so, yet another
funeral procession of funerals.
"sorry" "for" "your" "loss"
for the fat percentile
of flora + fauna being fed
through grinding teeth.

there are two perspectives to this:
one species plunges into brackish, foreign field—
    yet to the new, on the other side,
        blooms a plume of something not yet realized.

like how a planchette sees our faces
whirled, wheeling, a flurry of angles
through its nothing eye,

while we swear our fingers,
light as feathers,

haven't moved anything at all.

ornithomancy

the old woman tells me
she took a reiki master class
at the community college and now

she puts angel-themed bumper stickers on her corolla.
(THIS CAR IS PROTECTED BY ANGELS)
there is a dream catcher with plastic turquoise on the rearview window.

she says an angel guide told her
that feathers mean everything is okay.
if you see a feather, you should touch it.

after her father died there was
a pile of feathers outside of the bird feeder
and she knew he was in a better place.

i can only think of the bird
gutted, plucked, naked

dragging herself across the dirt
with a gut full of vomit and worm blood,
warbling a shriek at the claw marks.

her starving chicks in the nest —
their eyes locked behind flesh,
growing cold.

approaching him

after the body cooled like a leftover catering tray of eggplant parmesan,
after the skin sallowed and vellumed,
after the wax mold and the mold start,
after all orifices have been wired shut, metal spooled
through the gums and lips to suture the jaws closed,
after thorned contacts placed under the eyelids,
after layers of wood stain and gel have been applied to the face,
after hospital johnny thrown aside and replaced with suit,
after the slip into lacquered pine box, silk lined,
after the hands have been pried together and clasped,
only then do i approach him.

red lampshades, lily arrangements,
industrial carpet cleaner, soft and gentle
piano recordings, overworking air conditioner,
approaching him with my eyes closed and hands outstretched
like a victorian parlor game. approaching him is a pilgrimage,
crawling on high heeled shoes, then kneeling on mini pew,
approaching grief at an angle, in a labored procession,
hands up at my eyes, squinting blind at a colossal white beam,
only then can i touch him.
shudder at the chilled flesh, wrinkle-less, wan,
will be the first thing to go.

cemetery walk

entropy is the god of
death is the god of
entropy is the death of
god is the entropy of
death is the entropy of
god is the death of
entropy

my safety blanket. my baby.
my enemy to lover and back again.
my reflection. my pet poodle.

death, you calm befuddler!
the patient teacher an irate child chides
until blue in the face.

i pick up the empty nip bottles, mcnugget boxes, cigarette filters, plastic flowers. the garbage is filled with banana peels and natty ice cans. white petals sift on the veteran fields. powdered sugar on ice. violets. moss. dandelions. potted pansies. the drain water runoff greens a fertility. graffiti says "sad boy" on the cinder blocks. frowny face.

i feel no people.
even though they lay all around me.
a thousand dormant jack-in-the-boxes
with no crank, no calliope, no prank,
no reason for me to jump in fright.

the stillness crumples me.
the slow spill toward a cool horizon.

for now i'll savor the proximity
to anything at all,
before it collapses
once, finally, always.

mourning star

dove-gray earth
athena eyed
stone corpse

wanders its ellipse
in a wraith path.

dawn crowns like a clone
each day, the sun ferries up
her fire. her core a cathedral
of flares. exploding prayers.

the lantern beams down,
lamenting her dead,
revolving child.

heat bakes another layer
to the stasis. stillborn
wanderer is glass eyed.

craters thud, rattle the ragdoll.
kick of movement.
her cradle of grief
still blazing.

the bunker

through the radio static,
bleats a warning drone.
warheads are blitzing

through the border
toward our city center
filled with milk.

i know i should be in concrete,
but in my wooden shack
where i raise my baby
is all i can bear. her cradle of glass
frames her dreaming skull. dreams
that ring like a bell.

i can only think of her eyes,
curdling in the flash of heat.
pools of flesh, fused to glass.

so her grandmother, my mother,
who lives with us, in the wooden shack,
shucks her bones from her skin

as i drag stones, pluck hair,
gnaw off fingernails, pull train tracks,
roof tiles, shipping crates, my wedding ring,

rip my gold tooth, hammer it into
a ductile sheet. it hurts, we say,
it hurts like a mother.

sixty seconds. i place my baby in the pit
of miscellany. wrap her in the gold foil,
pack the soil, praying for alchemy

to turn it all back to lead. this is goodbye,

i tell her, thirty seconds.
she cries and cries and cries.

and i, under the husk of my mother,
writhe on the straw mattress,
thatch my ante-carcass into a mummy

for her, when she awakes,
to eat the mold from my shroud,
to wring a pulp from the spores.

the bombs huff,
and they puff,
blow the world up.

if i managed to cloister her properly, maybe
after millennia of dormancy,
she could cradle me,

what's left of me,

in her horrific arms.

protection

on the mountain top
laced with ice,
a stray oxygen molecule
drifts in the nose.

we can peel the nerve endings
from those mountains. leave pure
sensation. the brains in the vats,
we zap in the right spots, they think
they are climbing the himalayas.

who says every apex needs to be pleasurable?
don't you want to *know*,
just to know?

they call them little deaths.
explosions. mutually assisted.
no you hang up first. again,
ad nauseum, until the piles of fire
get to the point, where you just can't
hold it in anymore. even if you want to.
and a lot of times you don't. a lot of times
it's forced. it's a bunch of strange men
repeatedly pushing buttons far away until
the dirt has no choice but to burst.
the body betrays you, like it usually does,
with its decay and its hunger.

it didn't happen
when it happened to me, though.

when it happened to me,
i fell still
and in that falling,
became still.

the snow fell on
snow
fell on
snow.

traffic on everest

on the moon there is a garbage can filled with fake flowers,
emptied biweekly by the maintenance crew.

they're laid out by mourners
who are tourists, because all ritual
is spectacle, even grief.

at the clogged joints in the labyrinth:
frozen green boots, rigid rainbows,
a friend lost in the thin and ragged air

i hold my oxygen cylinder like someone else's child
who i'm saving from cannibal hunger,
whose busy blood cells traverse
their ancient trade routes
ferrying their fits and bursts.

a line of ants
on the edge of the sky,
stuck in their pattern
as more travelers
disembark, fistfuls of plastic,
ready to scatter.

the janitors wait in the crevices, bored.

wrath

i was voted "most likely to end up in heaven and be pissed about it"
in high school. just mad that i'd be wrong about it all.
but now i'd love to be wrong about the right thing.
every current event is just an unturned stone,
scattering beetles that hiss into darkness.

my anger is a furnace and its fuel,
a lattice of mule (masshole, connecticunt). concrete jungle.
and the last living monkey that is my one remaining brain cell
swings from jumper cable to jumper cable
over the abyss of broken, static-spewing televisions.

i scream constantly at every slow driver.
i get irritated by mistakes. as if a missed
turn signal could ever mar the sphere of stars.

my anger is in the boundless twelfth house,
spilling its alka seltzer coca cola feeding frenzy
across the martian sea.

i saw a red honda smack into a fat raccoon.
the thud of its death-whack like a canyon echo
but how can we save the rabid?
a fountain made of spit and blood. a ladle of bone.
one part bitters. one part sugar.
the rest, sea water.

furious meaning curious,
frustrated at the utopia beyond the brain pan.

hell is this
and only this:
an idea of heaven,
dangled, damoclean.
one big fat grape
clutched in the fist of a corpse.

burial burial

the warmed violin rosin of the funeral hall
soaked and heated oak in rose light
illuminates the baby blue plastic casket.

we've dug a hole for the worms
to laze around in, loping trapeze,
aerating for mycelia, who wait patiently.

her spiny body, meager and waxy,
a candle flickering itself to ruin.
red velvet carpet to quiet
the folding chair pews as we
up and down and up and down

the graveside is draped in astroturf despite
december and everything is snow.

we aren't to acknowledge
fleeting, sleet sluiced streets,
straw crops, leaking decomp.

the stand-still cork of it all,
vacuum-sealed bible verses.

preacher draws the bow
across the strings,
slices saturn's rings,
death rattle,
gathered here today.

saint judas

today's special offer   we have Saint Judas upended on the maypole

:: audience boos in unison ::

his tongue once slick
now scorched to charcoal from
the pure silver bridle we've stuffed in his mouth,
smoked in the crematory with a hundred dead fish.

he marinated in wine→
blood soaked the intestines,
through the pores for us to mop with bread→
flesh crisped in its aqueducts of fat,
stuck the peeled legs on a spit,
& spun them in infrared until the bile
wept its oily pearls onto the marble floor.

:: audience claps, impressed with the deal ::

but wait, there's more —
with a complementary solid flavor injector, we inserted
peeled garlic cloves into the muscle lodes,
to be sucked out of the wounds.

for dessert: sour apple granita shaved off lake cocytus,
drizzled with juniper syrup reduction,
served on a bed of thirty silver coins.

:: st thomas sticks a fork in him, and says *HE'S DONE* ::

:: audience is teleprompted a benediction ::

thank you, O Judas!
O blood-sucking angel!
for the gift of this dead lamb
roasted with vinegar and fly meat.

i love you Nosferatu, i love you Herr Vampyr!

:: audience feasts, lives forever ::

and now the carcass, its gristly leftovers
slung from the low branches.

when the bowels break,
poured onto the field :: offal to be scavenged ::
they'll coil at the foot of the tree:
        O the snakeroot!
        its poor perfume,
           screaming its smoke up to heaven.

i'm so glad i came but i can't wait to leave

i don't know if my last words are
ready for their close up, just yet.

their beautiful scrolls
wedged in my teeth

the roots pumping nutrients
to their meat

it's nice to
scrutinize them. it's nice

to be screwed. no taming.
mutiny of a shrew.

i make my barbital barbie doll
hump my seconal seneca

action figure. what,
no tongue? pussy cat.

eros and thanatos sitting in a tree
A B C D E F G

and in that string
my last words bide

in their own hidden system
like a lady in waiting,

in the grass. the cobra
unhinges its jaws.

tempt me, o socrates!
with your hemlock shots,

straight, no chaser,
actor, not receiver.

ötzi

his body - shriveled bug
of sinew, froze to stone,
by the ice floe's slow crawl.

bog of high atmosphere,
thin + clear, reveals
a tawny scapula, copper haunches.

amber + honey shellacked,
the bones crest through wax,
blood glows, in the deep recesses,

marbles of fire. blackened brambles.
set loose from the glacier's grasp
in 1991.

but last thoughts, still clogged,
in some far distant expanse,
far from his glass casket in tirol.

he + the world he was set in,
thawing in unison.
those last thoughts, impossible to render,

our flaming forked road. our heaven of bombs.
raining down our pompeiis
of bright snow, cocooning our gristle,

our leather bellies filled with ochre,
microplastics, cola syrup.

sepulcher after sepulcher
groaning in our wake.

the incredible shrinking god

the incredible shrinking god once was the whole world his edges were fuzzy like peach
and when you peered in close enough you saw they were fractals into nothing he
made a brilliant heaven where angels gave off their radiation he made heaven
hotter than he made hell in heaven the moon's the light of the sun and the sun
shines brighter than seven-day light 500 degrees kelvin is warmer than what
it takes to keep sulfur liquid heaven bakes the incredible shrinking god
too evaporating like crumbs from a communion wafer as his cavemen
just started to sniff out his existence form blueprint rituals from
blood daub it on cave walls with their fingertips painting
the stories of god deep in the dark that arrives at night in
the raw hearts purple and wet muscles that grow on
their own when you inflate a cervix with sperm the
baby starts growing is it growing or is that proto-
zoonotic goo just going through the motions
the incredible shrinking god set up so long
ago? same motions for planets ocean
wave ice peak rain fusion red raw
baby grows up to see the
world as a machine
free of miraculous
beings and
god shrinks
further down
to a pixel
for us
to observe
performs
on road
sides w/
cup for
change.

east

there is a plan
for the carcass to locust,
frog spawn the body pit.
to compost ghosts into air.

the sun sets - where, now?
west, as home of the dead.
necropoli of flare.
solar descension
we ride its orbit tracks
to a dark sky
riddled with stars,
like lice
or grains of rice.

but the plan - in the east -
a pure death scream,
potpourri of grief and ruin
with enough momentum
to grind earth on its heel,
pivot, reorient the death shroud
to set in the east.

polarity. apostasy. by any other name.

there are enough dead
to build a new city.
there are enough dead
to magnetize the star.

ΛΠSTRQ, they invert you.
your ostiarius betrayed,
leaks your innermost dawn.

we beseech you:
treat them well.

they, the soil in your breast,
they are your children.
at any cost.

your apostles —
hold their lamppost high,
as frost crawls in their nostrils
as their graves rotate
feet to the west.

east

there is a plan
for the carcass to locust,
frog spawn the body pit.
to compost ghosts into air.

the sun sets - where, now?
west, as home of the dead.
necropoli of flare.
solar descension
we ride its orbit tracks
to a dark sky
riddled with stars,
like lice
or grains of rice.

but the plan - in the east -
a pure death scream,
potpourri of grief and ruin
with enough momentum
to grind earth on its heel,
pivot, reorient the death shroud
to set in the east.

polarity. apostasy. by any other name.

there are enough dead
to build a new city.
there are enough dead
to magnetize the star.

ΛΠSTRQ, they invert you.
your ostiarius betrayed,
leaks your innermost dawn.

we beseech you:
treat them well.

they, the soil in your breast,
they are your children.
at any cost.

your apostles —
hold their lamppost high,
as frost crawls in their nostrils
as their graves rotate
feet to the west.

if loving the bomb is right, then we have to want to be wrong

after paul fussell

when the best we can do
is puzzlelock our horns
in a rat king of razors

then the moral imperative
is to reject. say thank you   no.
i would prefer not to. i'd rather

start again. with someone else.
we have to get off. we have to go.
it just isn't working out.

if the universe's orderly trajectory,
brick by combative brick, is an explosion
that boils the telephone polls to sulfur,
melts babies into mercurial pools,
drops the sun in the lap of shadows,
then it is no good.

we mean this sincerely.

no matter the path to this wreckage,
if the only way out is through colossal ferocity,
then pull the plug. drain the wound. staunch the flow.

if this is the only song the atoms sing, kill them.

all the roses in glass vases
all the meteor showers
all the hummingbirds and goldenrod and brook trout
are not worth the price of its totality.

when the meek lose paradise,
there is no higher calling,

no more courageous act
than forging a new god
from the corpse of the old.

human nature triptych

earth's first words were in german.

berlin olympics, 1936, first radio signal
to step across the stars,
powerful enough
to go where no man has gone.

einstein's last words were in german, too.

his nurse didn't understand the language,
and so the words slipped their meaning into waves.

the atoms in them, the atoms in me,
theirs, mine, ours, yours.

—

before and after
dust then human then dust
the prompt and utter destruction
the god damn potsdam.

how many people in the end would you
be willing to cleave in two, for food?
we become death and shock and awe
as splendid as the brightness of god.

planets, moon, and stars drop in his lap.
prophecy of euphrates, fulfilled and thank god.
fire at the end of the world, thank god.
cruel bombs, thank god, thank god.
thank god for nimble civilian shards
carved of plutonium afterglow.

through the ruin and rubble,
the apocalypse eats raw onions.

its teeth crunch cicadas in static,
talking into a dead end radio.

to be fair,
some will still want to sift
through the ashes + clouds
for their silver.

—

the world tilted blue,
little marble called mother,
sending sons into the dark.

apollo - god of light,
god of the plague,
destroyer of rats.

they shot his bow into the vacuum
pinned bodies in the sky.

magnificent desolation,
craters cracking the gunpowder.

view of the void,
alone in a module.

ancestors gazed at the light
as if a god, as if a soul, offering

their crops and their blood, and now
their progeny step upon its face,
looking down and back at us

what a pity, what a pity.

adam /// atom

once upon a time there was god and he was without a being in his image so he molded up a clay man sculpted of earth and huffed and puffed up his nostril the same way farmers inflate the lungs of silent calves he was the one formed from the ground *adamah* the same ground which housed the soil that the roots of the tree of the knowledge of good and evil grew adam's brain clear as spring water pawed at his ribs until god split him upon an altar *adam* meaning *to not cut* but god cut man and made woman and he pawed at her and she pawed back and when they had sex all the birds and the bees and the lions and lambs joined in and played with their bodies simply bodies no flesh to mend yet because no hissing scales wound up eve's legs and into her ear filling it with dreams of grandeur promises of angel gossip and leave it to god to make a forbidden tree bear fruit and leave it to god to plant a tree at all to let humans know and to make them fall out of grace forever when he could have easily just let us paw at each other and make happy babies with a smile and a breeze could have snapped serpents in two and bound their tongues with hyssop so when adam took a bite he was just pawing at fruit and became blistered with the knowledge of good and evil and knew his genitals were shameful and stuffed them with leaves.

adam and atom are made of indivisible things within which lie unspoken power and it took the earth-made man to split it in two *atom* meaning *to not cut* gets cut with the cleaver fashioned from snake fangs and skull shrapnel placed at each point like a tightly curled lotus by god for us to paw at and all the birds and bees and lambs and rocks and lions and babes are all made of this powerful thing and they all watch as the earth cuts up the earth and out comes the light let there be by god meant to flow out by god it's happening god static fast approaching oh god oh god they're coming to blow us off the face of *adamah* with their cut tongues and devil maws and oh god there's more stars in the sky than grains of sand on the earth but in each grain of sand and in each man lies enough force to throttle the heavens.

1997

hail mary, full of grace:
pray for us sinners.
phlegm of this earth
convulsion of this earth

i stalk across the sands like a vulture
sticking a straw into the eye socket of some
nameless foreign oasis.

i slurp the viscera,
and weep, for i know
exactly what i do.

tell me, mother mary
should i feel guilty for being alive?
every breath, a breath i mine
from the lungs of a child
who cherished the air
and deserved it more.

hail mary, heil mary,
flesh is barbaric,
        why didn't jesus
        snooze on the crucifix?
        why did he cry aloud?
                because he was still man!
                because he still had to pay
                the interplanetary toll!

hail mary, full of grace,
hale bopp, lace up
my death shroud.
scoop out my left eye with an ice cream scoop.

i'll wrap a crown of stinging nettles on my fists,
never get married and never have sex.

so maybe i can float to heaven
so maybe i can get vacuumed up
into the glass spheres of æther
and orbit the base core of the universe.

dear mary, i do in all honesty
hate this world.
devour sour grapes by the fistful,
turn them into water
(behold, the backwards son of god! pissing on the floor)

i've been dying every day, but it's harder to get gray
than to just get moving now.
i want to play for the away team.
i want to bat for fallen angels.

FOR GOD'S SAKE LET'S GET ON WITH IT!

out, out brief candle! smoke still stoked by empyrean glory
smoke oiled holy by the anointed
smoke snaking in the wake
of ultimate breath—

madonna lactans

on our doorsteps he dropped
mouse broth - eggshell crust,
sawdust bread - cricket aspic,
acid rain upside down cake.

the baskets overfloweth.
electric ozone cul de sac
sleep in shifts, the dawn
a shimmering limit to hit
arbitrarily, dawn after dawn.

raw sky chafes our skin
into sheets of blister. but
we couldn't resist. our babies:
forelocks curled with spit,
souls forged on charcoal,
the tantalizing petrol pumps.
their emulsified eyes bright.
lick the dead geese for oil.

when Charity came,
like a cockroach,
sprawled on the asphalt,
slouching across waste,
milk trailing from her breasts,
my baby latched her leech teeth.
her first word was
mama, manna, mammal

door to door, one at a time,
us bitter mothers with sour
glands handed them off,
cursing into our masks
as her body flowed and
flowed its river.

swear to god, i wanted to kill her.
out of jealousy, fear of the divine.

but it's my baby
who screams + grows,
hers stays clogged
in the dustbowl of her belly,
its stone lips curdled into stasis

while her body weeps its curds
and waits for a whisper
that has long since passed her by.

katabasis

a wiccan stripper with breast cancer photocopied the tibetan book of the dead at the library. she fed nickels into the little slot as toasty pages spilled out. i asked her why she didn't just check out the copy. "because i'm going to die tomorrow and there won't be anyone to take it back."

a lot of people became wiccan after the war. anthropologists called it *ecohysteria*. shamans considered mutually assured destruction as a blood sacrifice, allowing the earth to start over. a new mineral named *radiogardasonite* formed from the blasts and it cured a lot of people of the resulting illnesses. scientists hailed its genesis as a miracle, and proof of an interventionist god who loved us.

she said her daughter ducked and covered and calcified into a beautiful statue of the crystal. "it's amazing what the earth can do to heal itself. using corpses for medicine, genius." she ingested bits of her daughter's dead hand but this was years ago, she said, and the cancer's come back.

in the early days she was one of the few dancers who stuck with her career. her retinas were clear and she had no detached breast tissue. most women started working on having healthy babies or breeding hardier plants. she said the show must go on and civilization was first built to impress women. it would have to be rebuilt by the same motivation. but men wept as they watched her dance on a cinderblock stage.

she would remove her radiation suit bit by bit until she was bare, white blood cells singed in the exposure. she saved her coins like charon until she had enough to pay back her library late fees. she wanted to do something normal. and today her biological doomsday clock struck midnight and she knew she was going to die, so she used her wages to make copies.

"every day has felt like a reincarnation but tomorrow it will be the real thing. i think we'll meet again." she stapled the sheets of paper and walked out the door. i don't blame her for clinging to mundane traditions. i'd suffer through most anything to know that the inherited world is the same as i'd left it.

what we talk about when we talk about garbage

it starts as follows:
a baby bird falls into a brook.

i can only tell you what it's not.
it's not a mistake. it's not an accident.
it's not fate. it's not decided.
not a glitch. not an error.

the streambed bloodsucks its nutrients
back into the shifting soil. reverse mammary.
the earth nursing off its child. not a leech.
not a shark. not a sink. just the way.

fertilizer (i hardly know her)
i hardly know this earth's loam
from its trenches.
teeth can be seeds
when properly discombobulated
can be anything.

garbage by any other name...
maybe not in my lifetime,
but in time, for some life.

the supremacy of now is as confounding
as it is unfair. legacies as fallacy,
there is no reason the inevitable collapses
can't happen to me.

a few of my favorites. my trash is your pleasure.
my casket. bag of used coffee filters.
hearse. dump truck. baby bird.
used diaper. newborn fawn. sharps container.
sluice of dross. dew drop.
here we're all peers.

all we do is nature. the trenches.
the men that filled them. the lawns
that cover them. the nursing home
that neglects them. the thief who steals
them. the ambulance that chases them.

a hot towering cauldron of television screens,
styrofoam coolers, beach buckets, toothbrushes,
hair spray. trash heap babel. the seagulls

carry on carrioning. the vultures and the voles,
fat rats and flies, new and exciting amoebas,
impenetrable behind the order's veil,
in some far flung time.

all those eons and eras ago
when the sky hatched its asteroid,
boiled and blotted, out pops the
chittering head of a black-eyed rodent
nose shivering. the new dawn. the solar flare. the meek.

somewhere, in the innermost imaginings,
a better world becomes in our post-carbon image.
garbage on the mantle. on the altar. in the pocket.
in the armoire. on the banquet hall.

evolution rolls its one magic trick
into the mouth of a volcano.

the lava, regardless,
can only,
will only,
flow.

as above, so below

everything in the universe is either Baby, or Not Baby.

we took Baby to the cathedral
of velvet, propylene, abalone.
sirens sang on the altar
of gold bar
(*to have been
a king's crown
but in the kingless world
it was left to be*)
the baptismal font babbled on.

on the horizon, there was a fossil,
cracked open with a crowbar.
the waters of the rocks left tears
in the ground, isotopes of moses parting.

our lives of shit and water.
our deaths of gold and diamond.
the stars are helium, and cold,
ghosts of edelweiss, heliotropes, etc.

prayers sizzle upward
and wilt in the ionosphere.
no one on the other side
to collect their petals.
the yearning to metamorphosize,
now, while we can feel it, futile.

and besides, the stage is set:
Baby, crying.
Not Baby, field of stars.

two and a half minutes

the clock told me three things:
- this has happened before;
- it is happening again;
- and it is a miracle that we are not openly weeping in the streets.

i have just enough of a moment
to steep a cup of grapefruit oolong tea at 180*F.

i use the kettle my parents got as a wedding gift,
white metal with a blue rose on the side and a wooden handle.
it whistles and spits,
hissing its guts.

as the second hand pirouettes -
the hands, our hands.

it will be a lazy day
spent on the sofa
maybe we have books in our hands
or sip a beer
or wash a casserole dish,
the hands rotating soap-soaked sponge
over a stubborn splotch of dried tomato sauce.

and we will look out the window
at the same time —
see the glow begin,
feel its warm
total embrace.

maybe there is a split
second when we enjoy
coming together,
one.

the broadcast

breaking news...we can exclusively report...sodom and gomorrah have been flattened...completely destroyed!...my word...a mess...the first responders will be busy for...well it's just to clear the soot and radiation...we wouldn't want...yes let's make it clear that this...well deserved but my...how many...towers...let's go live to our man on the scene...now i've been instructed...not to turn around...the stench of brimstone...well here behind me are what once were...the cities...again we want to be clear...this was for the best...you can't even find ten...righteous...what's the point?...there were probably...babies...but they would have been raised by these...monsters...at that point...a mercy...we're told...there was an issue....of hospitality...holiness...the sulfur...acrid!...there will be well-trained volunteers ready...to clear it all away...rebuild...in our image...fig trees...baptismal fountain...tourist destination...next to this pillar...a warning of...the fierceness of fire...back to you.

dove and olive

There was a man named Oliver who discovered that he could physically manifest white doves. He only had to think of a dove and then touch his thumb to his front tooth. The first time it happened, he did it accidentally. He was thinking of the Prince song about doves and then felt a piece of spinach in his teeth. He went to wipe it away and then a white dove appeared right at his feet. With his gift he was able to become a well-respected magician and performed for kids' birthday parties. He didn't use his gift for the Greater Good until he saw on the news one day, that every confederate statue in America was replaced with a 7,777 year old olive tree. It happened overnight and no one knew why or how. They started appearing too in the Palestinian farmers' fields where Israeli soldiers torched the soil. So he decided to summon a white dove to hover over the shoulder of every world leader. It would not leave their heads and couldn't be killed by any secret service agents or other armed forces. Then one day he was at a Starbucks and heard the barista call for a Paloma, who ordered a venti caramel macchiato. He turned and saw the woman. He told her that that was a beautiful name. She said thank you and asked him his. He said Oliver. She smiled and they started to talk. They slowly realized that they each had a special, unique gift. Paloma could summon olive trees, and Oliver could summon white doves. They wondered what good fortune it was to have forces for peace as miracles in the world. He took her back to his house after feeling this instant connection and they had sex.

Paloma gave birth to a little baby boy. A blight came over all the olive trees and they withered on the spot. The people who depended on them starved to death. The world leaders all began to think that the white doves were part of a globalist conspiracy and went mad trying to bomb one another. Oliver and Paloma felt guilty for their meddling and laid down on the ground and let their bodies grow stale. Their baby had a gift too, and he could keep atoms completely still, freezing time. So he kept his parents as statues in the basement. He froze the whole world and then went looking under girls' skirts and touched what he found. But he didn't realize he couldn't unfreeze the atoms. He lived for eighty years in the barren, still world until he died from food poisoning, after eating a rotten olive from the one tree that had, up until that point, managed to escape all the magic.

the body parts

i held his head in my hands.
neck of broken arrows, cracked legs,
earthquake spine, phantom limbs for kindling.

i was painting his portrait during this sacred war,
one halo around his head,
another round the stump,
for a total of two, just to be safe
(i'm no expert on the soul)
but i know how holy it is to break and reform
as the earth gives birth to her dead.

i painted the haloes out of egg yolk and spit ... some grass
all we had in the field.
STAND STILL! i barked, i was the general in charge.
the inside of his recycled body continued to click
in the slick pink electric way it always did.
belly full of fish and loaves, particulate ribs,
echoes of hands, foliage innards, magpie body.

for a reference, i looked through the telescope
and peered at saturn retrograde...ice rings in a vacuum...of pressure...
a scholar once said...it could be...foreskin of the WORD MADE FLESH...
(sorry that you had to be one of us, to save us)...on the ascent to heaven...dropped it like a gum wrapper...and it clung to the hips...a gas giant...it feels like it could be a halo too...of ice and skin...*holy prepuce*...but what of Catherine?...wed to him...the bit invisible around her finger...a ring... sipping pus and nothing else...a feast? ... *anorexia mirabilis*... so full of the holy spirit that a crumb of the world becomes dead weight...so angels must drink light...lick clouds off each other in the brightness of GOD...wave and particle and particle and wave crest and trough frothing at the mouth a nothing beam of speed unbelievable illuminating a trinity let there be...

I CAN'T HOLD THIS POSE MUCH LONGER, he said,
botflies blooming in the wounds.
(catherine would have licked her lips,
if they had not turned to rose petals)

it was hard to tell what the maggots took
for their magpie guts...what was still his, him...

the body parts

i held his head in my hands.
neck of broken arrows, cracked legs,
earthquake spine, phantom limbs for kindling.

i was painting his portrait during this sacred war,
one halo around his head,
another round the stump,
for a total of two, just to be safe
(i'm no expert on the soul)
but i know how holy it is to break and reform
as the earth gives birth to her dead.

i painted the haloes out of egg yolk and spit ... some grass
all we had in the field.
STAND STILL! i barked, i was the general in charge.
the inside of his recycled body continued to click
in the slick pink electric way it always did.
belly full of fish and loaves, particulate ribs,
echoes of hands, foliage innards, magpie body.

for a reference, i looked through the telescope
and peered at saturn retrograde...ice rings in a vacuum...of pressure...
a scholar once said...it could be...foreskin of the WORD MADE FLESH...
(sorry that you had to be one of us, to save us)...on the ascent to heaven...dropped it like a gum wrapper...and it clung to the hips...a gas giant...it feels like it could be a halo too...of ice and skin...*holy prepuce*...but what of Catherine?...wed to him...the bit invisible around her finger...a ring... sipping pus and nothing else...a feast? ... *anorexia mirabilis*... so full of the holy spirit that a crumb of the world becomes dead weight...so angels must drink light...lick clouds off each other in the brightness of GOD...wave and particle and particle and wave crest and trough frothing at the mouth a nothing beam of speed unbelievable illuminating a trinity let there be...

I CAN'T HOLD THIS POSE MUCH LONGER, he said,
botflies blooming in the wounds.
(catherine would have licked her lips,
if they had not turned to rose petals)

it was hard to tell what the maggots took
for their magpie guts...what was still his, him...

theft of fire

for gus, ed, and roger

the moon god—
under worship by those neolithics,
who saw war in the red spark of mars,
never deigned to dream that selene
had a cheek we could step on.

what bold clay did Προμηθεύς carve
to give us the urge to launch into dark.

the gods speak in fire,
to moses, to the forests,
what did they say to the men drowning in sun?
repulsed by pure oxygen, melted into pools.
(why do you let us drown in what we are?)

their fused hearts, waxworks, feathers,
velcro, screams and burns, takes 90 minutes for
the melted nylon skin to peel.

every 90 minutes an eagle plucks their guts
from the metal seats, the circuitry, the fusion,
exposed electrical nerves, sparking like mars.

cabin lights blackened by dense smoke
whistling out the hatch, and yet
the moon has light enough
to flood the whole earth.

(what have you done?)

the gods gave us fire.
the gods gave us
too much.

ashes

at the flea market
on quaker meetinghouse road,

dust-caked folding tables hold
glass apocrypha from every

elderly household within a
five mile radius. empty tins

of ancient avon powders,
horseshoes of rust.

we vulturians pluck the
detritus for some lone,

valuable nutrient. a man
with a thick beard,

beer gut, muscle tee,
waves at me,

cigarette between his fingers
as i turn his wares over and

over. i find in his trove
an ashtray, white, untouched,

un-yellowed by smoke
and by time. Harry S Truman's

smiling, colorized face sits
in the pit like a bullseye.

i don't buy it. i don't smoke.
it's five dollars, the man says.

it's a collector's item. it takes
some restraint to keep myself

from yanking the cigarette from his hand,
collapsing its tower into the ashtray.

the smoldering tip does nothing
to blemish Harry S Truman's

smiling, colorized face. i would
take up smoking, just to torture

his ghost with the toxic clouds,
stamping out a flame in his eye sockets,

over and over,

until they are craters of soot.
but why waste my lungs

and their sacred gift

when i know that, if there is a Devil,
He is already doing the very same?

possum skull ode

the non-designed order of the possum's skull on my desk
brings me to insanity's solarium, where i totter around
in my wicker wheelchair with the rough linen blanket on my lap.

the asylum of order! the universe expresses itself
in the shape of a possum skull!

curious vacuum
curious calcium
o you furious gem

the shape of Secrets is a possum skull,
with flecks of flesh still stuck to the socket,
and i have fished it out of the dumpster.

who is the singer? the chorus of beheaded saints?
silent, but silence is only known since there is a song.

in you, possum skull, all things,
but who sings them?

the tower

i don't pretend to know
how these current calamities
will flow into each other, cancel
each other out, flow over scrolls,
leave their traces on dry river beds,
their doomed manuscripts, cracked earth,
soils depleted mote by mote.

i should be so lucky
to have my skull hollowed for a bowl
for my enemies to drink from.
or even crushed under boot.
i'll be whatever link in the chainmail
i can get.

flashes of rome in the mirror
as the green oil rolls down my cheek.
the ashes of future's past wait like daggers,
poised to strike, clenched tight in the fists
of ancestors, of progeny.

the blue sky, i know, is a pit
for clouds unyet seeded.
there's so much room to burst into fury.
bronze age afflictions ring like bells through the gun smoke

                              as the fiddle whimpers its pied piper lure,
            one cocked and beckoning finger,
settled on the bow.

the star

there are moments of sumptuous joy in the spanse of void,
heads of lettuce bobbing on the sea after the titanic capsized.

the needle in the haystack i use to piece my tongue —
a thread of silver linings stitching the wound.
strings of pearls hanging off my arms hit the ground
and snag and snap and roll,
far flung skitterings on a mirrored lagoon.

then the beast in the trees clicks its teeth,
rooting in the earth as if the jewels were turtle eggs —
scavenging the stars into its infernal firmament.

are there ever enough stars, enough pearls, enough silver spools,
enough iceberg lettuces,
are there enough to carry the yoke all the way to the punchline,
enough enough to be worth it?

No.

yet here we are —

collecting them, pouring our pitchers of clear cold water
into a never-ending pool.

would you believe me if i said
i'm still content to stay
in these black streams,
as long as you are?

the rock under isaac

the voice echoes still
       still echoes in the scrubland
the sandstorm electric air crackles the cells'
closed petal fists.

       if god wants you to feel it, you will feel it.

thrums of thunder,
aching blue sky,
perfumed by olive trees

and the stone
cradlecruciblepyre
upon which threads of sweat
run their rivers, while abraham
automates his angels,

the stone,
knowing nothing, and His nothing,
feels no lightning.

moves only,
       slightly, only when
the scriptures permit an errant atom
to slink away into a speck of sand,
into a fathomless stone ocean. where no whale eats.
where no fish multiplies. where nowhere dies.

the stone, alone, staid foundation
of a black, black eye,
dumb to every passerby, every offering,
laid across its brow
for the taking.

o, to have a pure stone mind!
       mantle of knowledge so deep,

the knowledge is unknown.

pax atomica

ye prophets of substance,
dismantling physical splendor,
seizing the chance to read god's mind
to feed starving babies
to power cities cleanly
to beat back cancers
to circumnavigate the heavens.

yet

in every joyous discovery,
in every utopian orgy,
there is the snake,
the neglected child,
the crippling thorn.
"*no matter,*" they said,
"*we'll smelt our swords
into the keys to heaven.*"

we know, now, those keys too
fit the gates of hell.

horrorstruck to gut
the cosmos and find
such savagery.

a meek little adam
    with enough force
        to unleash the winds of neptune.

they say again
"*we know not what we do!
we would have all been watchmakers
before we had BECOME DEATH!*"

too busy babel-building to think anyone would allow

the fission-steamed shadow of the thought cross their mind,
that one day, they'd splinter civilians into spouts of vapor,
grow clouds of supernova graveyards that rain white blasts of hot ash.

too busy babel-building
to care that it could happen again.

> *AND MEN WERE SCORCHED WITH GREAT HEAT, AND BLASPHEMED THE NAME OF GOD, WHICH HATH POWER OVER THESE PLAGUES: AND THEY REPENTED NOT TO GIVE HIM GLORY.*

letters from the final frontier:
    [a minute past midnight]

we shelved our radioactive breast milk because the sores on the cows were too much.
we walked on a brand new land bridge.
the snow glowed
as it fell.
it was so quiet
when it fell
on the motionless fossils of my family.
i lit some candles with my breath, splitting
the billows of smog to scavenge for cores, seeds, meat.

but there's a smile on my face, because we are united.
one twitch & the world was aflame &

in the rubble, i asked the charred fractures of bone
if knowing god
is worth killing for?

[   ]

can you believe how smooth the world feels in your palm?
polished robin's egg.
hollow and blue,
not a pulse in sight.

HOW LONG, O LORD, HOLY AND TRUE, DOST THOU NOT JUDGE AND AVENGE OUR BLOOD ON THEM THAT DWELL ON THE EARTH?

TO: the human race, remains
RE: accident

here we were with our wonder-welling eyes. but on behalf of my brethren, i'd like to apologize for any emotional damages our actions may have caused. we thought that for once we could salvage some harmony from the discord. but we were wrong and again we apologize for our blind-eye optimism, the spitfire lab rats, and any subsequent victims in the pursuit of understanding god's numb tongue. we don't blame him for the quiet, but you know what they say, curiosity killed the cat. maybe if he had laid out a clearer sign, told eve *why* she shouldn't eat of the tree, rather than just shouting no...i digress. to any of the offspring: we've planted bombs that will last into eternity. only a small cache was launched to bring this about. there are plenty more indecipherable toys for you to play with when you inevitably discover them scattered like seeds in a barren wasteland. bash at them with sticks and stones if you like and start the whole thing over again. they'll ring like an echo from time. but what difference does this rambling make, your language will be unrecognizable. and i'm scrawling this apology with spit through the dust on my skin. exercise in futility. but maybe i'll mummify, and one genius among you will see this eulogy, thumb your nose at the sky, and tell god that the lions and lambs finally laid down together, but only after their shadows were smeared on the concrete. yours, truly.

angelus novus

and i look back, the tears of my eyes,
pearls of god. i am a river of their weeping.

i am the
steward / stillbirth / testimony / hiccup / spectrum
of this desolation.

the hospital burns like a burst furnace.
the moon is quiet. yes, it is quiet.
the kindling shrieks - a foaming rapid.

ash-covered mice leave ribbons in the soot.
black snakes of negation. the prints of
raccoons / rabbits / deer / dogs / foxes
are to be swept into mounds by the hulking wind,
its towering breath, acrid with creosote.

my daughters climb the hill. my husband
cannot look them in the eyes.

of course i dare, and ache,
the vats of gore bloating my heart
to a fevered flood gate,
the seems creaking with the weight
of each slaughtered granule.

i couldn't follow them, if i wanted to.
and the beauty, and the horror, and the miracle, and the burden,
is that i will never want to.

this earth is an
orchestra / orchid / corpuscle / thunder / crescendo

orpheus, my god, it is worth it.

sméagol's elegy

always for the poor creatures devoured by the mountains,
their roots of stone; their hidden pools of black sunless water;
a clutch of my eggs in their throats,
clogging them, choking them, sputtering,
>   even their names blurred to a hacking snarl
>   because, sometimes, i am a destroying angel.

pity the worm on a rusted hook, being mocked by wise fish.
pity the asteroid crumbling to a speck in the æther.
pity the shivering leaf, last to fall from the branch.

the line between pity and mercy is impossible to see with the naked eye.
you have to call its name three times in a mirror. give mercy to the executioner.
mercy to a bombardier. mercy to the monsters and the venoms they spew.

mercy to those who cling to power because they are afraid of death. mercy to death.
pity to lady macbeth. pity mephistopheles. mercy to those who waste their one life in
the cesspools of fear and chaos. pity to those who never have a chance again to learn,
and see that all they do is shadow.

>   and yes i guide my prayers like missiles
to the scoundrels of this earth. all my life i got mad at the platitudes,
they seemed so hollow to the victims, the survivors. but if on the death bed
of a demon, an angel can appear, hold up a mirror and
burst them by the pain of the light,
then who am i, destroyer, to judge? who am i to stop my mercy from saving the world?
>   o lord forge my heart into a pity chamber.
>   i can salvage the wretched there.

i wield my pity and my mercy like swords
even when i don't mean to.
i want my blood to boil like lava at evil.
but, at best, it will only ever flow,
and swallow all deeds.

the last oasis

throw my last breadcrumbs into the pond
frog chorus chants aqua-hymns
spawn scum ripples in moonlight

the ducks have died out
and this fecund pit groans
under the weight
multiplying tadpoles
mitosis mother dividing

i miss having birds, and wind, and breeze,
i hate these rotted mosquito sores
humid with eggs and croaks

the sky buzzes thunderheads
cracks open and slimes
like a yolk
from the clouds,

everything is thick.
i miss being delicate.

mary at nagasaki

her bruised peach face,
stone made soft by the

blast of heat. she stares
blind, from the pools of

dark ash. a gift to have
your eyes plucked by

the vultures of neptune,
riding the winds of fire.

why would anyone, even
She, want to witness

the burst tomato skin,
infant flayed into vapor,

roasted hearts, the clots
thick, drip on the splinters,

bone shards pierced
shadows into place

like a veil of mourning
pinned to the nape?

why would any
One do any

thing any differently?
in the blank of Her

eyes, the dirt,
rootless, can

flow like tears
over the bodies

of her murdered
children, and cover

them with soil so
sacred, no eyes
could bear the sight.

SISENEG

The Cherubim dips his flaming Sword into the Euphrates,
sparkling Waters hiss at the Heat.
He sheaths It,
ascends into Heaven,
leaves the Tree of Life undefended
but They aren't afraid.

G-D takes away uterine Pain,
peels Snake Skin off His Sons' Heels.
no Sweat or Thistles or Thorns.
Death disappears for Now.

Eve places her Fig Leaves back on the Branch,
to collect Sun. Adam returns the Fruit,
One She has not offered at all.

The Serpent coils into the Brush, becomes Quiet.
Semen loses its Sin,
We regain the Knowledge of Nothing.

Eve's Body shrinks
into a Bone Fragment,
slips into Adam's sleeping Heart.
Beasts shed Their Names,
become wild Mysteries of Earth.

The Tree of the Knowledge of Good and Evil
rescinds Its Seeds,
unsplit and unfurled.
Rivers dry to winding Paths,
lush Gardens shrink.

The Tree of Life stands,
its Mystery forever unaffected.

G-D vacuums Adam's Breath away and

He falls back into Dust
like a Dream being forgotten.

the Heavens shudder their Spectacles,
Birds and Waters and Stars and Planets and Ground,
revert to formless Deep.

G-D removes the Light,
lets Darkness be.

He becomes still over the Waters.
Nothing happens Here.

about the author

Lindsey Frances Pellino is a poet and artist from Connecticut. Her first collection of poetry, *HYSTERICAL SISTERS*, was published by Vegetarian Alcoholic Press in 2018. Her work has appeared in ANON Magazine, Breadcrumbs Mag, and YES Clash.

www.ingramcontent.com/pod-product-compliance
Lightning Source LLC
Chambersburg PA
CBHW041325110526
44592CB00021B/2829